ROCK & ROLL
HALL OF FAMERS

The Supremes

URSULA RIVERA

the rosen publishing group's
rosen
central

To Stephen Dominic D'Agostino: a true music lover, a true friend

Published in 2002 by The Rosen Publishing Group, Inc.
29 East 21st Street, New York, NY 10010

Library of Congress Cataloging-in-Publication Data

Rivera, Ursula.
The Supremes / by Ursula Rivera. — 1st ed.
p. cm. — (Rock & roll hall of famers)
Includes discography, filmography, list of Web sites, bibliographical references, and index.
ISBN 0-8239-3527-2 (library binding)
1. Supremes (Musical group)—Juvenile literature. 2. Women singers—United States—Biography—Juvenile literature. [1. Supremes (Musical group). 2. Singers. 3. Women–Biography. 4. African Americans—Biography. 5. Rock music.] I. Title. II. Series.
ML3930.S9853 R58 2002
782.421644'092'2–dc21

2001004185

Manufactured in the United States of America

CONTENTS

With tremendous talent and determination, the Supremes became one of the most influential vocal groups of all time.

Introduction

On January 20, 1988, the Supremes were inducted into the Rock and Roll Hall of Fame in Cleveland, Ohio. Mary Wilson was the only member of the Supremes present that night. Florence Ballard had died in 1976; she was represented at the ceremony by her daughter, Lisa Chapman. Diana Ross was unable to attend. The ceremony that night took place more than twenty years after the Supremes' greatest hits had been recorded. Still, the group continues to have an enormous influence on performers to this day.

There are many girl groups that have followed in the Supremes' footsteps. En Vogue, Destiny's Child, SWV, the Go-Go's, the Bangles, and even Salt 'n' Pepa and TLC owe a great deal to the style and charisma of the Supremes. The Supremes represented a breakthrough in pop music in the United States and all over the world. For the first time, audiences of all races were singing along with black, female singers. The Supremes influenced more than just music; they affected fashion and hairstyles, product endorsements, television, and film.

Through music, the Supremes broke down racial barriers at a time when many states remained strictly segregated. Segregation ensured that blacks and whites were separated. Separate schools and even separate public rest rooms existed for whites and blacks. The Supremes entertained fans of all races, however. Audiences everywhere responded to their class, their beautiful harmonies, and their toe-tapping tunes.

The Supremes paved the way for other popular female vocal groups, like Destiny's Child *(left)* and the Go-Go's.

They proved that black women were strong and deserving of the same rights and respect as any other human beings. In the United States during the 1950s and the 1960s, the thought that these young, black performers were equal to successful, white musicians was revolutionary.

At the high point of their career, the Supremes were the number-two pop music group in the world, second in popularity only to the Beatles. They had fans in England, Switzerland, Africa, Germany, France, Japan, Hong Kong, and dozens of other countries. In June 1965, the Supremes set the record for the most consecutive number-one hits on the *Billboard* pop charts (they charted five in a row). During a five-year period, they had twelve number-one hits! They inspired, entertained, and thrilled generations of music fans with their talent, beauty, and energy.

This is the inspiring story of the Supremes. Florence Ballard, Mary Wilson, and Diana Ross came from humble beginnings. All three of them worked tirelessly to achieve their success. When everyone else thought their music careers were a long shot, these three young women believed in their dream. Through years of rehearsals and dozens of tours that took them to racist towns and run-down motels, the Supremes stuck it out. They were determined to succeed, and in the end that's exactly what they did.

It's also the story of three friends who struggled with personal difficulties. Though each woman had struggles in her own life, each managed to focus on the same end result. Even though the friends grew apart over the years, the Supremes maintained their incredible success. These three young women struggled to go after the one thing they loved most: singing. Though they experienced personal and professional difficulties along the way, they really did make their dreams come true!

Three Kids from Detroit

In Detroit, Michigan, during the 1950s, soul music and rhythm and blues (R & B) were thriving. There were plenty of clubs where black musicians like Dinah Washington, Nat "King" Cole, and Ray Charles appeared regularly. Though the United States remained segregated in many ways, black performers were beginning to have success with audiences of all races. As these performers achieved success on the white pop music charts, they became known as "crossover acts" because their music was appealing to wider audiences and crossing over boundaries of race and musical tastes.

The young women who became the Supremes all shared a similar background. Ballard, Wilson, and Ross were from large families, with parents who struggled to make ends meet. Their families instilled in the girls a drive to succeed and a willingness to work hard for what they wanted to achieve.

The Brewster Projects

The city of Detroit was an empowering place for many black families to live during the 1950s. Automobile factories provided plenty of jobs for hardworking men and women. Black parents were able to raise families in middle-class

Did You Know?

The Supremes recorded on the Motown label, which also represented other extraordinary artists. Marvin Gaye, Stevie Wonder, Mary Wells, and Martha and the Vandellas were all Motown recording stars. Together these black musicians stormed the pop music charts and changed music history forever.

neighborhoods, and they had access to good schools and housing.

When they met, all three girls were living in the Brewster Projects in Detroit. Like many public housing projects, the Brewster Projects developed a reputation for crime and danger, but when Mary, Flo, and Diane were young, it was still a safe community for many families. It wasn't a perfect life—there were street gangs and a lot of poverty—

but it was an affordable option for many families that were struggling financially.

Mary Wilson

Mary Wilson was born on March 6, 1944, in Greenville, Mississippi. Her mother, Johnnie Mae, worked steadily when Mary was a baby, but her father, Sam Wilson, had difficulty

In the fifties, Detroit, Michigan, was a bustling, industrial metropolis.

holding a steady job. The Wilsons moved from Mississippi to St. Louis, Missouri, and then moved again to Chicago, Illinois. In Chicago, Sam Wilson became involved with gambling and did not pay much attention to his family. By that time, Mary had a younger brother, Roosevelt, and Johnnie Mae was forced to ask her family for help.

When Mary was three years old, she went to live with her mother's sister, I. V., and I. V.'s

Mary Wilson's household was filled with the sounds of Nat "King" Cole and Sarah Vaughan.

husband, John Pippin. The Pippins lived in a small house in Dearborn, Michigan. Mary was still very young when she went to live with her aunt and uncle, and she grew to think of them as her real parents; soon she called them Mom and Daddy. Mary's brother, Roosevelt, and later her baby sister, Cathy, lived with Johnnie Mae and Mary's grandmother back in Greenville.

Mary's aunt I. V. was very interested in fashion and beauty. Mary grew up sharing these interests and was always very well dressed. John Pippin worked two jobs to support his family, but in his spare time he enjoyed listening to popular singers. He listened to jazz and R & B vocalists like Nat "King" Cole, Sarah Vaughan, LaVern Baker, and Brook Benton. Mary soon grew to love music, too.

When Mary was six years old, her mother, brother, and sister came to live with the Pippins in Dearborn. By this time, I. V. and John had a daughter of their own, Pat. Though it was difficult for Mary to understand at first, she soon learned that Johnnie Mae, not I. V., was her real mother. Though the family got along well, the house was too small for seven people. Johnnie Mae took her three children and moved to the Brewster Projects in nearby Detroit.

Mary's love of music continued, and sometimes she found the courage to sing in public. When she was in junior high school, Mary entered a school talent contest. Backstage, she met the girl who was to become her best friend, Florence Ballard, who was nicknamed Flo. The girls connected instantly. Mary recalled, "We promised each other that if either of us were ever asked to join a singing group, she would call the other. There was a bond between us. We could not have known that it would last a lifetime."

Florence Ballard

Florence Ballard was born on June 30, 1943, in Detroit. She was the eighth of thirteen children born to her parents, Jesse and Lurlee Ballard. Like the Wilson family, the Ballards had moved to Detroit from Mississippi. Jesse Ballard worked in an automobile factory and Lurlee ran the busy household full of kids. For many years, the Ballards lived in a large house near the Brewster Projects. After Lurlee gave birth to her last child, the Ballards moved, joining the Brewster Projects community.

Once Mary and Flo became friends in junior high school, Mary spent a lot of time hanging out at the Ballard household. In her autobiography,

Mary Wilson recalled that the Ballard family was a very close one. In such a large family, there was a big age difference between the oldest and youngest children, but they all pitched in and shared everything in their busy home. Like Mary, Flo grew up listening to the music that her parents played. Her father, Jesse, was a gifted singer and guitar player, and he taught his children to sing. Flo loved to sing. She sang songs from the radio with her friends and sang in school choirs. As Flo grew older, people recognized her talent. She was known for having a strong, soulful voice.

Diane Ross

Another friend from Mary and Flo's junior high school days was Diane Ross. Born in Detroit on March 26, 1944, Diane was the second child of six. Diane's father, Fred Ross, held several jobs to support his large family. Diane's mother, Ernestine, took care of the children and worked part-time jobs to make ends meet. One of Ernestine's jobs was cleaning a movie theater. While her mother cleaned, Diane would sit and watch bits of

Diana Ross, then Diane Ross, during her high school years

movies as the projectionist was preparing the films. Watching the movies had a big influence on the dreams Diane had for herself.

Young Diane, like Mary and Flo, enjoyed singing and performing. As a child, she performed for her family members, doing song or tap dance routines. She was an athletic tomboy who enjoyed riding her bike, swimming, and running. As a youngster, Diane was competitive and had a real drive to excel at the things she loved doing. Mary later said of Diane, "She was always very energetic and talkative. I really admired her. In her I found a missing part of myself, a more aggressive side I could never express comfortably."

Diane was also a music lover. Her childhood idol was the blues singer Etta James. Inspired by James's emotional voice, Diane dreamed of becoming an entertainer. She said, "Singing became my life. I lived, ate, drank, and breathed it. It was all that I cared about. I had a dream, and I was completely determined to make it real. Nothing could deter me or discourage me for very long."

When Diane was fourteen years old, the Ross family moved to the Brewster Projects. Though she was the same age as Mary and Florence, Diane did not attend the same school as the other two girls. Diane attended Cass Technical School, where she was required to keep a B average to remain at the school. Diane kept her grades up and focused on the classes she loved, including fashion design. She had a knack for making her own clothing and was voted best-dressed student during her senior year.

Getting It Together

Long before graduating from high school, things began happening for Mary, Florence, and Diane. In 1959, when Mary and Diane were fourteen years old, Flo asked them to join her in a singing group. Florence was friends with a men's singing group called the Primes. The group's manager, Milton Jenkins, asked her to form a sister group to perform with the Primes. The women's group would be called the Primettes. Mary and Diane were thrilled and agreed to be a part of the group. Together with Betty McGlown, who was dating one of the Primes, the girls became the Primettes.

Flo, Mary, and Diane also had to get permission to be part of the group. Since singing was something that would keep them out of trouble, the girls had little problem convincing their parents. When the girls agreed to get their schoolwork done in addition to rehearsing the music, the girls' parents allowed them all to participate.

None of the four girls could read music, so they had to learn the songs by ear. The Primes worked with them, helping them polish their four-part harmonies and teaching them dance moves to go along with their songs. The young women performed together naturally and loved it from the beginning. They rehearsed every day.

Flo usually sang lead vocals in the early days. Her strong, bluesy voice was similar to other singers of the time. Diane had a much higher, nasal voice that was still untrained. Mary and Betty sang wonderful harmonies. With plenty of practice, they really did sound good together. Before long, the girls were making appearances as the Primettes.

1959

Flo asks Mary, Diane, and Betty McGlown to join her in a singing group called the Primettes.

1960

The Primettes audition for Berry Gordy Jr. of Motown Records. He tells them to come back after they graduate from high school.

1961

The Primettes are signed by Tamla-Motown Records. They change their name to the Supremes.

1962

The Supremes tour the southern United States as part of the Motortown Revue.

1963

The Supremes release their first single, "When the Lovelight Starts Shining Through His Eyes," written by Holland, Dozier, Holland (HDH).

1964
The Supremes join Dick Clark's Caravan of Stars tour.

1965
The Supremes tour Europe for the first time, and the group's name is changed to Diana Ross and the Supremes.

1968
The group films the television special *Taking Care of Business* with the Temptations.

1969
Diana Ross announces that she is leaving the group.

1970
On January 14, the group performs their final concert at the Frontier Hotel in Las Vegas.

The Primettes

The Primettes first appeared at a local union meeting. They rotated lead vocals so that each girl was featured on at least one song. The audience responded with a lot of applause for the girls' performance. Milton Jenkins was pleased and started booking the Primettes at other events.

In the beginning, the girls sang covers

of hit songs they knew from listening to the radio. Local DJs would play recorded instrumental tracks with which the girls sang along. Soon, the group met Marvin Tarplin, an acoustic guitarist who knew many of the songs they performed and could read music as well. The Primettes could now perform with a live musician in addition to prerecorded music.

It wasn't easy, though. Flo, Diane, and Mary had only just graduated from the eighth grade when they became members of the Primettes. Along with singing, they were dealing with new high schools. Diane had started her studies at Cass Tech, and Mary was attending Northeastern High with Flo. Betty lived in a different part of town and went to a different high school. All four of the girls were planning to go to college, so they knew that studying was as important to their lives as singing. They all worked hard to strike a balance between the performing that they loved and the studying that they had to do.

As the group got more gigs, Diane and Mary decided that the Primettes needed a more sophisticated look. They wanted to try designing their own stage dresses. The first gowns that they made for the Primettes were orange floral balloon dresses that puffed out at the waist and tapered at the knee. It began a long tradition of the girls appearing in cutting-edge fashions.

No Stopping

The Primettes had dreams of recording for Motown Records, the famous company founded by Berry Gordy Jr. Before they had the chance to audition for Motown, they had released a record on a small label called Lupine. The songs they

Fun Fact!

Before their first public appearance, Milton Jenkins's girlfriend took the Primettes shopping for outfits. The girls agreed that their look should be clean and classy. They chose to wear letter sweaters and pleated skirts with bobby socks and sneakers.

recorded for Lupine were "Tears of Sorrow" and "Pretty Baby." The songs were recorded in 1959 and were supposed to be released that year. Unfortunately, financial problems caused the record label to fold and the songs remained unreleased for many years.

In 1960, the girls continued to perform frequently, often at weekend sock hops or festivals. Their manager, Milton Jenkins, began to focus on other groups and eventually stopped working for the Primettes altogether. This didn't stop the energetic young women. They had spent weeks rehearsing four-part harmonies and dance moves, and they had spent hours creating dresses from scratch. They weren't about to let the loss of a manager stop them now. The Primettes had enough of a reputation that the girls were able to book performances on their own. When they could, they appeared at events at one of the high schools or at parties. They kept focusing on new music, too.

Flo briefly dated a young man named Jesse Greer, who was a member of another singing group, the Peppermints. Though Jesse and

Flo broke up, they remained friends, and he helped the girls rehearse new material. He taught them to perform harmonies like some of the successful men's groups of the time, such as the Mills Brothers.

Canadian Contest

In the summer of 1960, a radio station in Windsor, Canada, held a contest for performers from both Canada and the United States. The Primettes were convinced they had a good chance to win. With great excitement, they asked their parents for permission to attend the contest. Unfortunately, Diane's father wasn't enthusiastic about the contest. Fred Ross was concerned that Diane spent more and more of her time singing. He was worried that she was neglecting her education and might be compromising her future. Despite Diane's arguments and tears, her father refused to let her attend the contest in July. The other Primettes, however, found a way to save the day. They spoke with Diane's parents and explained how important the contest was to all of them. Finally, Fred Ross agreed to let Diane go.

On July 16, 1960, the Primettes took the stage in Windsor, Canada. They felt upbeat and excited about their performance that day, and the audience responded by dancing and singing along. There were thousands of people in attendance at the contest, which featured many other talented acts. The time came to announce the contest winners and, sure enough, the Primettes took the grand prize! The girls were thrilled. They spent the rest of their visit at an amusement park and accepted congratulations from people who had seen them perform. Their guitarist, Marvin Tarplin, suggested that the Primettes should audition for Motown Records when they got back to Detroit.

The Primettes Meet Motown

Following their success in Canada, the Primettes decided to see if they could land a record contract with Motown. They already had a small connection to Motown: before Diane Ross's

Motown

Detroit has long been known as "the Motor City" because it is a center of production for automobile companies. Berry Gordy Jr. used that nickname and gave it a twist by calling his record company "Motown." Motown was also commonly known as Hitsville, U.S.A.

Berry Gordy Jr. was a successful young boxer when he was in his early twenties. After serving in the U.S. Army during the Korean War, Gordy returned to his hometown of Detroit and opened a record store. When that business fell apart, Gordy worked at an auto factory, but he also began pursuing songwriting. The singer Jackie Wilson had a hit with a song that Gordy cowrote, called "Reet Petite." Gordy continued writing for Wilson, and he soon found success writing for the Miracles, which featured his good friend, singer Smokey Robinson.

Gordy used his songwriting successes to begin a record company called Tamla. Within a year he was successful enough to start a second label, which he named Motown Records. The list of stars that recorded for the Motown label is incredible: Mary Wells, the Temptations, Marvin Gaye, Martha and the Vandellas, Stevie Wonder, and many other chart-topping artists.

family moved to the Brewster Projects, their neighbor had been Smokey Robinson of the Miracles. By this time, the Miracles had already had a hit song on the Motown label, and the Primettes decided their best bet was to ask Robinson to help them out.

The Primettes sought out Smokey Robinson to help them land a deal with Motown Records.

The Primettes met Robinson and the other Miracles during a rehearsal. They performed their usual songs, featuring both Flo and Diane on lead vocals. Robinson was friendly and supportive, but he seemed most interested in Tarplin, who was playing guitar. Robinson asked if he could borrow Tarplin for a few Miracles sessions, and the girls agreed. Unfortunately, Marvin never played for the Primettes again!

Losing their guitar player to Robinson's group was a letdown, but the girls refused to give up. Marvin did what he could for them, and recommended the group to one of the sound engineers at Motown. Through that engineer, the Primettes managed to schedule an audition with Berry Gordy Jr. himself!

The First Audition

Late in the summer of 1960, the Primettes sat waiting for their audition with Berry Gordy Jr. Soon they were led into a recording studio and asked to sing the songs they had prepared. The girls were very nervous, and they had to sing a cappella since they no longer had Tarplin to accompany them on guitar. After the girls sang four songs for Berry Gordy Jr. and some other Motown producers, Gordy asked them how old they were. They replied that they were seniors in high school.

Berry Gordy Jr., founder of Motown Records

Gordy thought carefully before giving them his answer. It was clear to him that the girls were talented and ambitious, but it was also clear that they were very young. He politely told the girls to finish high school and then come see him again.

It wasn't the answer the Primettes had hoped for, but they thanked Gordy and left. The rejection didn't stop them. Once school started in the fall, the girls met every day at the Motown offices right after classes. Diane remembered, "We could hardly wait for school to get out so we could ride the bus to that building every day. Everybody at Motown got used to seeing us; we quickly became permanent fixtures there." Though they were not allowed to record vocals, they got the chance to do background handclaps on some tracks. Watching professionals, the Primettes were able to use what they learned and polish their own act.

The Primettes also began working with Richard Morris, the engineer who had set up the audition with Gordy. Morris got Gordy's permission to work with the Primettes on his own time, without offering them a contract. He also started acting as the group's manager and began booking them at more events in the Detroit area.

Working through their new contacts, the Primettes got better and better gigs. They were able to open for successful entertainers like Wilson Pickett and Johnny Mathis. With each performance, the Primettes felt more professional and ready for their own recording contract. In less than a year, the girls would have the contract they had been dreaming of.

From Primettes to Supremes

The months that followed the Primettes' first Motown audition were not easy ones. Though the girls agreed to meet each day at the Motown studio after school, it was hard to stay focused on what they wanted to do. Schoolwork and boyfriends were distracting all four girls.

Betty McGlown was the first to

leave the Primettes. Betty had always looked at
the group as a fun thing to do, but she had other
dreams for her life. When she fell in love and
decided to get married, she left the group. The
remaining Primettes were sad to lose Betty, but
they were determined to continue. Since the
harmonies they sang were in four parts, it was
important for them to find a replacement singer.
Through one of Flo's teachers, the girls met
Barbara Martin. Barbara was enthusiastic and
had good chemistry with the other three
performers. She began showing up at the
Motown studios with the other girls each day.
Before the Primettes could focus on practicing
with the new singer, though, Flo mysteriously
stopped coming to rehearsals.

A Terrible Event

At first Diane and Mary were confused by Flo's
disappearance. When they phoned her house,
Flo refused to speak with them and her mother
told the girls that Flo had decided to do other
things. Neither Diane nor Mary could

believe this, since Flo had been the founding member of the group. Flo was determined to make the Primettes a success, yet it seemed that she was ready to quit the group!

It was several weeks before Flo finally contacted the other girls. When they met in person, Diane and Mary were shocked that Flo seemed like a different person. Her usual bubbly energy was no longer there and she seemed deeply depressed. Diane and Mary begged Flo for details, and she finally told them the truth. After attending a sock hop with her brother, Flo got separated in the crowd and couldn't find her brother's car for the ride home. An acquaintance from the Brewster Projects pulled up in his car and offered her a ride. She accepted, even though she didn't know the man well. Before she knew it, he had driven to another part of town and had forced her into the backseat at knifepoint and raped her.

The experience broke Flo's spirit. The Ballard family closed in around her, protecting her from anything and anyone that might disappoint her. That included the Primettes. Over the following weeks, the girls began to rehearse again and Flo seemed to return to her old self. In their memoirs, though, both of Flo's singing partners remembered that she was never quite the same after the attack.

Trying Again

The girls returned to Motown in late 1960. They had been away for several months, but the other artists welcomed them back with open arms. Mary Wells asked them to sing backup on some of her recordings. The girls were thrilled. Berry Gordy Jr. stressed that this was not a contract; the Primettes were only performing backups on a few tracks.

The recording sessions with Mary Wells were successful, although not all of them were released at the time. Slowly but surely, the Primettes began working with other artists at Motown. Finally, Smokey Robinson decided to help them record songs of their own. The first

Mary Wells had the Primettes sing backup on some of her songs.

song they recorded at Motown was a cover of the Miracles' song "Who's Loving You?" Diane sang lead, and the other three sang backup.

At last, Berry Gordy Jr. agreed to sign the Primettes to a recording contract, but he had two conditions. First, he was signing them to Tamla, his older label that was not quite as famous as the Motown label. Second, he didn't like the group's name. The girls would have to decide on something other than the Primettes.

Flo kept track of all the possible names they came up with: the Royaltones, the Jewelettes, and the Supremes. There were many others, but Flo was most taken with the Supremes. Though none of the other girls felt as strongly about it, they agreed to go with Flo's choice. In January 1961, the Supremes were signed as recording artists with the Tamla label!

First Releases

At last, the hardworking quartet would have a chance to have their music released! They had been disappointed when the Lupine songs hadn't been sold to the public, but their patience and hard work had paid off. The Supremes went into the studio to record their first single, "I Want a Guy." Diane sang the lead vocal, and this began to set the pattern for future recordings. Many people still preferred Flo's strong voice, but Berry Gordy knew that Diane's voice was unique and would sell records.

Diane's voice had matured over the years and was less nasal than before. It was still a very different singing voice from the voices of the other female artists recording at Motown at the time, though. Gordy hoped that Diane's sound would help the Supremes stand out from the other artists. He was right, but it took a long time for radio listeners to catch on.

There were still some opportunities for Flo to sing lead. On the Supremes' third single, "Buttered Popcorn," Flo sang the sassy lead vocal, but Gordy's decision to feature Diane more than the others was already in place. Still, the release of their songs meant that audiences were more familiar with the group when they performed, and the girls remained excited regardless of who was singing lead.

Did You Know?

The Supremes' first public performance after signing with Motown was opening for Gladys Knight and the Pips. The girls were nervous and frightened of performing with a strange band. The results were disappointing, and the girls left the stage in tears.

The Supremes recorded four songs for the Tamla label. Gordy then had a change of heart and transferred the group to the more prestigious Motown label. The Supremes began a busy schedule of performances, often opening for better-known artists. The Supremes gained more confidence and took their new success in style. Encouraged by other Motown artists, such as Gladys Knight, the girls felt more comfortable playing to larger audiences and got used to new routines.

And Then There Were Three

Despite a heavy weekend touring schedule, the Supremes were still in school all through 1961. Diane, Flo, and Mary were now high school seniors preparing for graduation. In October, Barbara Martin announced to the group that she was pregnant. The other girls were shocked; Barbara wasn't married, and they didn't know how the situation would reflect on the group.

After thinking things through, Flo and Mary decided it didn't matter, and Barbara agreed to stay as long as she could. Diane believed differently. She felt certain that the Supremes could make it as a trio. Eventually, Barbara's pregnancy forced her to cut back and she left the group. By 1962, the Supremes were a trio.

They weren't a very successful group, though. Audiences around Detroit knew and loved the Supremes, but their records were not getting much radio play. The group had earned itself the nickname the No-Hit Supremes to the girls' embarrassment. Still, they focused on their dreams of success. They continued to record new singles and to tour.

The Motortown Revue

In November 1962, the Supremes joined other Motown artists on a tour called the Motortown Revue. The revue was notable because it toured through southern states where segregation was still a reality. In the places the tour was headed, blacks still had separate water fountains and bathrooms, and they were forced to sit at the backs of public buses. At first, Gordy did not want the Supremes to go on the tour because

The Motortown Revue was an opportunity for the Supremes to strut their stuff and hone their live act.

they were so young. Diane Ross talked him into letting them go. She was determined that the Supremes get as much exposure to new audiences as any of the other Motown artists.

When the girls had traveled in the past, they were often accompanied by one of their mothers. For the Motortown Revue, Gordy made certain the Supremes had a chaperone. The chaperone's

The Supremes got a great response at the famous Apollo Theater in Harlem, New York, at the end of the Motortown Revue.

job was to make sure that the Supremes were protected from sexual advances and that they acted like ladies.

Even with a chaperone, the trip was a hard one. Flo, Diane, and Mary experienced racism as never before. Diane later said, "In some of those Southern towns, you could just feel the bigotry in the air. You could slice it with a knife like stinking cheese." Despite the progress of civil rights laws, there were plenty of towns that ignored the law. In some towns, sheriffs with dogs confronted the performers. After one performance, someone fired gunshots at their tour bus! Fortunately, no one was hurt. Though Motown's music was slowly breaking down some barriers, it was clear that for much of the country, racism was still the norm.

The highlight of the tour was the final concert at New York's Apollo Theater. The Apollo was a famous concert hall for black performers. The audiences could be very cruel; if they didn't like a performer, they would boo until the emcee pulled the act off the stage with a giant hook. The Supremes had no problem impressing the New Yorkers and left the stage with the audience cheering for more!

The First Hits

In December 1963, the Supremes' first album, called *Meet the Supremes*, was released. The album included "Buttered Popcorn," "Let Me Go the Right Way," and "I Want a Guy." Through 1963,

the Supremes continued to tour, and three more singles were released, including "A Breath Taking Guy." Still, no Supremes song could be considered a hit. The girls kept working, with the hope that something would catch the ears of nationwide radio listeners.

Berry Gordy Jr. was also concerned about the Supremes. He hired songwriters specifically to create the hit song the group needed so badly. As part of this songwriting effort, Gordy hired a trio of cowriters: Brian Holland, Lamont Dozier, and Eddie Holland, who were known as HDH. HDH had written hits for Martha and the Vandellas, including "Heat Wave," and Gordy felt sure they could do the same for the Supremes.

The first HDH song the Supremes performed, "When the Lovelight Starts Shining Through His Eyes," went to number twenty-three on the pop charts. That was the most successful of any Supremes song to that point, so the girls felt encouraged by its success. Their next HDH song, "Run, Run, Run," was a dud, though, and their spirits fell.

The Supremes' first hits were penned by the team of Holland, Dozier, and Holland (HDH), pictured here in 1990 with Diana Ross.

Only Room for One

Gordy made a decision that Flo and Mary had suspected was coming all along. He told the group that Diane alone would sing lead vocals. The other two would sing backup. This also meant that Diane would no longer sing backup vocals, so the three-part harmonies the group had spent years perfecting were now reduced to only two parts: lead vocal and backups. It was a disappointing moment for Mary and Flo. Mary recalled, "Besides being upstaged, Flo and I also felt that the records suffered; our three-part harmonies were so beautiful; we should have recorded more of them."

The first song the Supremes recorded under the new arrangement was written by HDH. "Where Did Our Love Go?" was a song that none of the Supremes were wild about when they first heard it. Mary thought the song was too childish. Flo thought it didn't have enough soul. In fact, the song had first been offered to the Marvelettes, so the Supremes felt like they were getting another group's leftovers. At Gordy's insistence, the Supremes recorded the song.

"Where Did Our Love Go?" was recorded in June 1964, and the following month the Supremes left Detroit to join Dick Clark's Caravan of Stars tour. When the tour started, the Supremes were an opening act, playing before

Did You Know?

Diane's mother, Ernestine Ross, went along on the Caravan of Stars tour as the girls' chaperone. She was so loved by the other performers that she earned the nickname Mama Supreme.

other performers that already had hit songs. As the tour progressed through the summer, "Where Did Our Love Go" climbed higher on the charts. Each evening, more audiences knew who the Supremes were and could sing along to their new hit song.

As the tour bus traveled from town to town, the girls had the thrill of hearing their hit played on the radio. Their slot in the lineup for the show got better at each gig, and by the end of the summer they had the number-one song in the country. As the tour finished, the Supremes were no longer the opening act—the Supremes were the headliners!

Hit After Hit

In September and October of 1964, two more HDH songs were released and went straight to number one on the pop charts. "Baby Love" and "Come See About Me" had the same unique sound as "Where Did Our Love Go?" With a catchy, driving beat, Diane's cool lead vocal, and the backing vocals of Flo and Mary, the sound of these songs caught the ears of fans all over the world. Even though the Supremes had not been crazy about these songs to begin with, they knew they had something good going.

Motown artist Mary Wells surprised everyone by switching record labels. Wells had been scheduled to headline an international Motortown Revue tour of Europe in October, but now it looked as if the tour would have to be canceled. Instead, Gordy decided to keep the tour going by sending the Supremes as headliners. The three young ladies from the

The Supremes found themselves headlining Motown's European tour.

Brewster Projects were on their way to meet British royalty!

Touring Europe

The Beatles were all the rage in the United States when the Supremes headed for England. Giant crowds of fans drove themselves crazy whenever the Beatles arrived in the United States. The Supremes had no idea of what to expect when they got to London. Would the English audiences appreciate the Motown sound?

It was an incredibly big step for three young, black women from Detroit to get their passports and fly off to Europe. Since they were headliners, they flew first class. No more tour buses and ratty motels for these girls!

The Supremes had nothing to worry about. Huge crowds of fans greeted them at the airport. Everywhere they went, the Supremes were interviewed and photographed and treated kindly by their hosts. While they were touring England, "Where Did Our Love Go" went to number two on the British charts.

A special treat occurred when the Supremes were invited to stay at the home of Lord and Lady Londonderry outside of London. For a week, the three performers stayed at their hosts' English mansion. Each evening they took a limousine from the Londonderry estate to the concert hall, then returned again after the show.

Audiences flocked to see the Supremes.

The British soul singer Dusty Springfield was
a big fan of Motown. She convinced the British
Broadcasting Company (BBC) to film a
television show about the tour. Springfield
hosted the special and performed with the
Motown guests. The show also featured the
other Motown artists on the tour: the
Temptations, Stevie Wonder, the Miracles, and
Martha and the Vandellas.

Berry Gordy and his family were traveling
with the tour as well. Gordy had big dreams for
all his artists, and he used the tour to work with
the Supremes on an unusual jazz arrangement
of the pop standard "You're Nobody 'Til
Somebody Loves You." The song was difficult to
perform, but Gordy felt it would show that the
Supremes had a range that was wider than their
catchy HDH tunes.

The first time the Supremes performed "You're
Nobody 'Til Somebody Loves You," the audience
didn't know how to respond. The song was so
different from "Baby Love" and "Come See About
Me." Diane felt that the audience hated the song,
and she was angry with Gordy for forcing them to

perform it. In the end, though, Gordy was right. As the Supremes got used to the new arrangement, audiences began to like the song more. It opened the door for the Supremes to begin recording other new songs that were not in the HDH style.

In the years to come, the Supremes would take great advantage of this newfound range. They recorded albums of Broadway show tunes and tributes to jazz musicians, composers, and other performers. They even recorded a country and western album!

Diana and producer Berry Gordy fell in love.

A Quiet Romance

As the tour continued on to Germany and France, the Supremes were greeted by adoring fans at every stop. They experienced an acceptance from European audiences that was quite unlike the reception from the segregated audiences they had seen on their tour of the southern United States.

Behind the scenes, Ross and Gordy were beginning to fall in love. When the tour reached its final destination in Paris, France, Gordy told Ross that he loved her. Initially, Ross replied that it would be better if they remained just friends. She didn't want anything to distract her from focusing on her career. Gordy was persistent, though, and by the tour's end, Ross and Gordy were involved in the beginning of an on-again, off-again romance that would last for many years. Though both of them would eventually date other people, they remained very close.

More Success at Home

The success of the international Motortown Revue tour led Gordy to pursue other performance opportunities for the Supremes. Early 1965 brought more number-one hits for the group, including "Stop! In the Name of Love" and "Back in My Arms." By early summer, Gordy had made arrangements for the Supremes to appear at the Copa, a famous nightclub in New York City.

In the meantime, the Supremes had a full schedule. In May, the group recorded two commercials for Coca-Cola, singing to the tunes of "Baby Love" and "When the Lovelight Starts Shining Through His Eyes." They taped television appearances on *Hullabaloo!* and an ABC special at the Hollywood Palace. The Supremes appeared on the covers of *Time* and *Ebony* magazines.

Gordy wanted to be sure that everything was perfect for the Copa appearance. To prepare for the show, he booked the Supremes at a much smaller club in New Jersey called the Rip-Tide. At the Rip-Tide, the Supremes rehearsed new routines each day and then performed them for audiences at night. They were able to find what audiences liked and what they didn't like and changed the show daily. By the time the Supremes opened at the Copa on July 29, 1965, they were ready for superstardom!

Troubled Times

The Supremes' appearance at the Copa in New York City was a smash. Their hours of rehearsals and trying the show out at the Rip-Tide paid off in a big way. Critics loved the show, and its success brought even more attention to the three busy entertainers.

During an interview that autumn, Diane announced that her name was now Diana Ross. Flo and Mary later claimed they had never heard about this, but she was referred to as "Diana" in the liner notes of the Supremes' first album. Flo and Mary continued to call her Diane, but to the public she was now officially Diana Ross.

More Changes

The name change signaled other changes as well. Diana and Gordy had been very discreet about their relationship, but most employees of Motown knew about their affair. Flo and Mary didn't oppose Diana's relationship with Gordy, but it did mean that she had more access to the man who was in charge of their careers. This caused some friction, since it was apparent that Diana was becoming a solo performer and Flo and Mary were thought of as backup singers. Still, the Supremes stuck together as their careers got even hotter.

Following their huge success at the Copa, the Supremes were booked to play other clubs all over the country. Through the remainder of 1965 and well into 1966, the group continued to release hit singles and albums. "I Hear a Symphony," "You Can't Hurry Love," and "You Keep Me Hangin' On" all went to number one. The Supremes released six albums in 1965 alone!

Not all of the albums were equally successful. Some of them featured special material, like their Christmas album and a tribute album to musician Sam Cooke. The success of the hit singles pushed everything else forward, though. It seemed the group was truly unstoppable.

Busy Life

The Supremes' schedule in 1966 was almost unbelievable. After a return engagement at the Copa in early March, the group recorded six new tracks and appeared on television on *The Sammy Davis Show* and *The Dean Martin Show.* They also did a weeklong appearance at a club in Boston and launched an ad campaign for a brand of white bread—all before April 1!

Later that year, the Supremes appeared on many television shows and specials, including *The Ed Sullivan Show, The Today Show, The Mike Douglas*

The Supremes maintained a busy schedule of TV appearances, recordings, and performances.

Show, and *The Tonight Show*. They made regular concert appearances in Virginia Beach, Virginia; San Francisco, California; Atlantic City, New Jersey; Forest Hills, New York; Los Angeles, California; and Miami, Florida. They toured the Far East, visiting Manila, Tokyo, Okinawa, and Hong Kong. They gave interviews to dozens of magazines, hosted parades, and recorded new singles, live albums, and a tribute album to the composers Rodgers and Hart.

The schedule was frantic and proved very hard for the three women. For weeks at a time, Diana felt too nauseous to eat. Her weight dropped, and she looked skinny and sickly during television appearances. She recalled, "I was becoming skin and bones, and eating became repulsive. It was a very unhappy time for me. Although the Supremes were at the top, I often felt as if I were sitting at the bottom of a deep, dark pit." Flo reacted to the stress by drinking heavily. As a result, her weight increased and she had difficulty fitting into some of the tighter costumes. The alcohol also fueled Flo's jealousy of Diana, which was increasing as the lead singer got more and more public attention.

More Tension

Without consulting Flo and Mary, Gordy made a dramatic decision. The group would no longer be known as "the Supremes." Instead, Diana was now publicly presented as the lead singer, and the group's name was changed to "Diana Ross and the Supremes." The tension between the women increased. "The real meaning of changing our name to 'Diana Ross and the Supremes' became clear to me as I looked across the room at Berry and Diane," Mary later said of the change. "All of a sudden, I was alone. There wasn't a group anymore. This was the worst thing that had ever happened to us, yet Diane and I would never speak about it."

Diana and Mary knew that Flo's drinking was becoming a problem. They tried to help by cutting back on their own drinking, hoping that Flo would get the hint and drink less. They tried hiding Flo's drinks from her. Nothing seemed to help. In the 1960s, alcoholism was still considered a dirty secret. It was not talked about openly. There was no way to get Flo the help

Cindy Birdsong *(far right)* was brought in to replace Flo Ballard.

she needed at the time. Instead, Flo continued to drink, started showing up late to public appearances and rehearsals, and continued to feel hurt and angry. Things got even worse when Gordy confronted Flo about her weight. She responded by throwing a drink in his face. Gordy lost patience with Flo's behavior.

A Supreme Replacement

In 1967, Gordy told Mary and Diana that he was searching for a singer to replace Flo. Cindy Birdsong, a member of Patti LaBelle and the Bluebelles, had often been told that she looked a lot like Florence Ballard. Gordy was considering Birdsong to be the next Supreme.

In the spring, Flo showed up for a performance so drunk that she had to be sent home. Diana and Mary performed the show by themselves. Flo continued to make appearances with the Supremes, but on April 29, Cindy Birdsong made her first public appearance as Flo's stand-in. In May, Flo made her last television appearance on *The Tonight Show*. In July, she appeared tipsy at a performance in Las Vegas. After a backstage argument with Gordy, Florence Ballard was no longer a Supreme.

The following night, Cindy Birdsong stepped into the Las Vegas show and replaced Flo for good. Strangely, audiences didn't seem to mind the change. Since Birdsong actually did look like Flo, many people didn't realize the switch had been made until it was announced to the public. Birdsong was also a good performer. She learned the routines and harmonies quickly, and Mary and Diana were both comfortable with her. Diana Ross and the Supremes charged ahead as though nothing had happened.

Moving Forward

The group continued its demanding schedule. In September, Diana Ross and the Supremes made their first television appearance with Cindy in the group. In October, their greatest

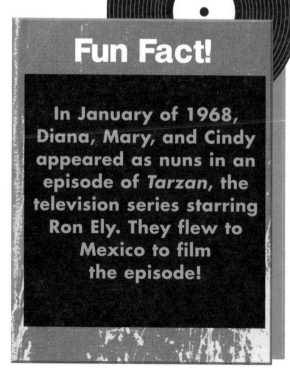

Fun Fact!

In January of 1968, Diana, Mary, and Cindy appeared as nuns in an episode of *Tarzan*, the television series starring Ron Ely. They flew to Mexico to film the episode!

On their second European tour in 1968, the Supremes met the queen of England and other royalty.

Tragedy

On April 4, 1968, Dr. Martin Luther King Jr. was assassinated in Memphis, Tennessee. The news was devastating for the Supremes. They canceled their scheduled engagements at the Copa in New York and flew to Atlanta for the funeral. King's widow asked the Supremes to perform at a rally in the days that followed King's burial. Along with several other Motown artists, the Supremes performed at the Atlanta Civic Center as part of the Poor People's March from Atlanta to Washington, D.C.

Dr. King's death was a turning point in race relations in the United States. The nation had watched as King and his followers staged a series of nonviolent protests to oppose racial segregation in the United States. After his assassination, many people no longer felt they could simply watch from the sidelines. While protesting King's death in grief and despair, many people rioted in major cities, including Detroit.

The Supremes began feeling some pressure to voice political opinions in interviews. Times had changed and many in the black community felt it was not enough for the group to be positive role models for young black women. The sophisticated image the Supremes had worked so hard to maintain was sometimes ridiculed by people who suggested the group wasn't "black enough." Though the Supremes never publicly stated political opinions, they did show their support for civil rights causes again and again. Indeed, since their earliest days in the Motortown Revue, the Supremes had worked hard to level the playing field for black performers.

hits album went straight to number one. Before Thanksgiving, they completed more recordings, guest spots on *The Ed Sullivan Show,* and live appearances in Oregon, Washington, California, and Canada.

In January 1968, after working right through Christmas and New Year's, Diana Ross and the Supremes began another European tour. Again they dined with dukes and duchesses, in between recording television specials in Amsterdam, Madrid, Paris, London, and Munich!

Even with Cindy in place, things were still difficult for the group. In February 1968, the song "Forever Came Today" was released. Strangely, none of the Supremes sang the song except Diana Ross. The studio had kept the recording date but did not book Mary or Cindy for the backing vocal tracks.

The release of "Forever Came Today" was the first time this happened, but it wasn't the last. As the group's schedule got more complicated, future recordings focused more on Diana's vocals than on using the group as a whole. If Mary and Cindy were not available to record, other singers recorded in their place. All the songs were released under the name "Diana Ross and the Supremes," and Mary and Cindy still had to learn the songs in order to perform them live.

Left Out Again

Later in the year, Mary flew to Los Angeles to look for a house. She decided to relocate to the West Coast in reaction to the Detroit riots that followed Martin Luther King Jr.'s assassination. While she was away, Gordy pushed through the recording of a new Supremes single, "Love Child." The song was written and recorded in a very short period of time and, though Cindy sang on the track, another singer was brought in to cover Mary's part.

Mary was not surprised by the event, but she was disappointed. As she had learned with the recording of "Forever Came Today," Gordy was concerned about the recording schedule before everything else. Other recordings began to feature Mary and Cindy less and less, while focusing on Diana's solo sound.

End of a Dream

In the fall of 1968, Diana Ross and the Supremes began working on the first of a series of television variety specials. Gordy had contracted the group to do a series of three specials, working with TV producer George Schlatter. Schlatter was a talented producer who brought out the best in the musicians and performers who worked with him. He was particularly good at directing comedy, and he helped Diana and the others with their acting in the short skits they performed.

Taking Care of Business

The first special was called *TCB: Taking Care of Business*, with Diana Ross and the Supremes and the Temptations. The production looked amazing. A great deal of money was spent to make sure the groups looked good, sounded good, and kept the audience happy. At the beginning of *TCB*, Diana, Mary, and Cindy appeared on a giant see-through stage. A full orchestra was conducted behind them, and a live audience was seated around the stage, which was shaped like a stop sign.

All three women looked amazing, wearing bright, sequined gowns designed by Bob Mackie. Mackie was a designer who made clothes for many female stars at the time, including Cher. In addition to the gowns, each of the Supremes wore a perfectly styled wig and glamorous

TCB was a great success for the Supremes and the Temptations.

makeup. After singing their introductions, the Supremes were joined by the Temptations, who appeared in crushed-velvet suits.

TCB was proof of just how far the Supremes' sound had crossed over. Diana and the Supremes performed only pop tunes in the special—no jazz, no R & B, and no blues were included. They performed a lot of Broadway tunes. Since the

Supremes now sang pop exclusively, some critics continued to accuse them of ignoring their soulful beginnings. In contrast, the Temptations continued to sing songs that were very much in the tradition of soul and R & B.

Diana was definitely the featured performer on *TCB*. In addition to her musical numbers with Mary and Cindy, Diana had many solo parts. During her first solo, she sang the Beatles' "Eleanor Rigby" while wearing pink satin pants and a vest with a big ruffle. She was also featured in a dramatic African dance number. Diana did not sing during the dance, but she whirled about the stage in different African costumes. *TCB* made it easy to understand why Gordy focused so hard on Diana's talents. She really stood out from the rest of the group. It was not only because she was the lead singer. Diana Ross had very special gifts as a performer. She was able to connect with audiences in a unique way. The preparation and money that had been poured into *TCB* were well worth it. The special received very high ratings when it aired on December 9, 1968. The sound track album to the show went to number one at the same time.

Beginning of the End

Though *TCB* succeeded by featuring Diana Ross, the same was not true within the Supremes. Diana continued to separate herself from Mary and Cindy as much as possible. The Temptations felt neglected during the filming of the special and were angry about the special treatment Diana received as the star of the show.

Though the Supremes recorded more singles, including "I'm Livin' in Shame," Mary did not perform on the songs. The singles were not successful. Critics said that they did not sound like the Supremes any longer.

Diana's solo appearances on television and in interviews happened more frequently. She appeared as a guest on *Laugh-In*, a TV comedy show. She also appeared on a special with Lucille Ball and Dinah Shore. In interviews, she began telling people that she was leaving the Supremes and planning her solo career.

Still, no official announcement had been made. The group was still under contract to Motown and still had television specials scheduled. Diana, Mary, and Cindy were still "Diana Ross and the Supremes" even though they weren't spending much time together.

Winding Down

In October 1969, Diana Ross and the Supremes hosted a TV special at the Hollywood Palace in Los Angeles. Diana was the hostess of the show, which featured comedian Soupy Sales, Motown's Stevie Wonder, and singer and actress Ethel Waters. Waters was famous for being the first black actress to appear in a dramatic play on Broadway. Diana sang a touching musical number with Waters, showcasing the two talented black performers from different generations. Diana was also featured in another dance segment.

This TV special was followed by another variety show from the producers of *TCB*. The 1969 special was called *G.I.T.*, or *Getting It Together*, with Diana Ross and the Supremes and the Temptations. The formula for the show was the same as *TCB*, although this special was filmed in a real Broadway theater. Again Diana, Mary, and Cindy sang covers of Broadway tunes. Again the Temptations performed more traditional R & B and funk numbers. The special included many skits and many solo spots for Diana. The costumes and hairstyles were extravagant.

G.I.T. was not as successful as *TCB*. The two groups had lost their spark. Diana was now thought of as an independent performer. Her focus was on her own career. In fact, Mary and Cindy were already rehearsing with Jean Terrell, a singer who had been hired as "the next Supreme." Though no one had announced it yet, Diana Ross was going solo.

Even Motown was not the same. Berry Gordy had moved to Los Angeles, and he was in the process of moving the company's headquarters as well. Though the house known as Hitsville U.S.A. still stood in Detroit, it was no longer the center of activity for the record label.

Someday

Not surprisingly, the group's last single was recorded without either Mary or Cindy. "Someday We'll Be Together" was a bittersweet

Did You Know?

On December 2, 1969, an intruder attacked Cindy Birdsong in her Los Angeles home and forced her into his car at knifepoint. Cindy escaped by opening the door and jumping out of the moving car. She was injured and bleeding but soon recovered. Her attacker was arrested the next day in Las Vegas.

song of regret, looking back at life gone by and looking hopefully for a future reunion. Still, it was a sad ending for a group that had struggled so long and come so far.

Diana Ross and the Supremes made their last television appearance together on *The Ed Sullivan Show* in mid-December 1969. They performed their last live concert together at the Frontier Hotel in Las Vegas on January 14, 1970. It was a poignant night for all three women. The audience was supportive and cheered them on for more than an hour. Mary sang solo on "Can't Take My Eyes Off of You." Diana moved through the audience welcoming Motown performers and their families and encouraging the audience to sing along with the Supremes.

When the evening was over, it was the end of a dream. The Supremes were still Motown recording artists, but only one founding member remained. Mary Wilson was determined to continue the group, but she was tired and sad. She missed the early days when Flo, Diane, and Mary had been excited young performers. She thought Jean Terrell was talented, and she had grown close to Cindy Birdsong, but Mary knew that it would be tough for the group to find success again.

Diana's Success

Diana Ross plunged into her solo career without looking back. The first solo single she released was "Reach Out and Touch (Somebody's Hand)." She often performed the

Jean Terrell *(center)* took Diana Ross's place in the Supremes in 1969.

song as an audience participation number in her concerts. In July 1970, her second single, "Ain't No Mountain High Enough," shot to number one.

In January 1971, Ross married Robert Silberstein. In August, she gave birth to her first child, Rhonda Suzanne. The focus of Ross's life changed as she concentrated on

After the Supremes, Diana Ross enjoyed a tremendously successful solo career.

being a mother and a wife. She began to investigate acting projects, including the life stories of Billie Holiday and Josephine Baker.

Her research paid off. In late 1971, Diana began filming her starring role in *Lady Sings the Blues*, the life story of Billie Holiday. It was a demanding role. Billie Holiday was a talented blues singer, but she was also a drug addict, and the movie portrayed the harsh realities of her life. Diana was rewarded with an Oscar nomination for Best Actress the following year. Though she didn't win the award, it was clear that she was a very talented actress.

In the years to come, Diana would continue to challenge herself with new musical challenges and movie roles. She had great success with starring roles in *Mahogany* and *The Wiz*, a remake of *The Wizard of Oz*, costarring a young Michael Jackson.

Supremes Continued

Surprisingly, Mary Wilson did not want to step forward as the new lead vocalist for the

Supremes. The group could have gone back to rotating lead, the way they had done in the old days when Flo was still a Supreme. Instead, the newest Supreme, Jean Terrell, took over Diana's spot as the lead vocalist. However, the group's name remained the Supremes.

With Jean in place, the Supremes wasted no time in appearing publicly. Just one month after the farewell concert in Las Vegas, the Supremes appeared with the new lineup on *The Ed Sullivan Show.* It was the first time they performed their new single, "Up the Ladder to the Roof." Audiences were receptive, and the single did very well on the charts.

As they had done in years past, the Supremes kept up a busy schedule of touring, television appearances, and interviews. Though critics were mixed about the new sound of the Supremes, many fans stuck with them and supported them through the change.

Not Forgotten

To the surprise of many people, the Supremes continued to be successful after Diana Ross left the group. With Jean Terrell singing lead, the Supremes began a new phase of their careers. Mary, Cindy, and Jean toured heavily to support their first album

To the surprise of some, the new Supremes, post–Diana Ross, still did relatively well during the 1970s.

together, *Right On*. The album featured a new sound for the Supremes.

On *Right On*, the group sounded more soulful. There were more group harmonies like in the old days of the Supremes. Audiences responded positively to the new sound, and the group continued with a second album, *New Ways . . . But Love Stays*. That album featured an even funkier sound and included covers of songs by the Beatles and Simon and Garfunkel.

More Bumps in the Road

Though they were off to a good start, the Supremes had new problems. Mary Wilson was disappointed in the way Motown marketed the new Supremes. Though the group did have successful singles, she felt the company was ignoring their albums. Mary thought Motown was making poor choices when designing album covers. As she had learned over the previous fifteen years, the Supremes' image was as important as its performances.

The music business had changed a lot as well. FM radio had created a much broader listening audience, and people had more choice about what they listened to. The Supremes were still known for their greatest HDH songs, like "Where Did Our Love Go?" If a listener didn't like the HDH songs, it was hard to get them to tune in to new Supremes material.

The Supremes themselves had personal distractions as well. Cindy Birdsong had gotten married in 1970, and in 1972 she was pregnant with her first child. She had decided that she would not return to the group after the child was born. After searching for a replacement, the Supremes found Lynda Laurence, a young singer who was thrilled to be part of the act. Both Jean and Mary felt comfortable with Lynda and were hopeful that things would work out, but there were more problems to come.

In the summer of 1972, Jean Terrell began having health problems that kept her in the hospital for weeks at a time. Though Cindy was several months pregnant, she came back to help the group get through an engagement at the Copa in New York City. Then Mary fell ill, so the New York audience saw a show that featured Cindy, Jean, and Lynda. For the first time, the Supremes had put on a show without any original members of the group.

Mary was depressed by all of this. She was grateful to Cindy for agreeing to help out, but she was sad that the Supremes had become a group in which the members were interchangeable. Still, Mary was determined to stay true to the Supremes.

Supremes Come and Go

The Supremes continued to record albums through 1977. They made many attempts to experiment with new music, producers, and sounds. Sadly, they were never again as successful as they were when Flo, Mary, and Diana were singing HDH songs.

The Supremes' lineup continued to change through the '70s. After Lynda Laurence became a Supreme, Jean Terrell left. Cindy Birdsong came back and a new singer, Scherrie Payne, joined. Cindy left again and was replaced by Susaye Green.

It was too confusing for fans to follow. People lost track of who the Supremes were, and they stopped listening to the music. Though Mary Wilson stuck with the group through thick and thin, she spent years sorting through legal problems with Motown Records. Eventually, the Supremes' long life as a group was finished. Mary Wilson became a solo artist, as had Diana Ross.

Florence's Tough Life

After Florence Ballard left the Supremes in 1967, she faced some tough times. She received payment from Motown for her participation in the Supremes, but the payment agreement prevented her from ever suing Motown for royalties on her past recordings with the group. At first, Flo started a solo recording career with another label. Her husband, Tommy Chapman, was Flo's manager. She performed gigs at small clubs and bars, and she even got a chance to perform at President Richard Nixon's inauguration festivities in 1969.

Flo's family was growing, too. She gave birth to three daughters and tried to support her large family with her earnings from her music career. Unfortunately, Flo's lawyer told her that all of her Motown earnings were used up. She accused the lawyer of mishandling her finances but was never able to prove it. Many years later, the lawyer was convicted of mishandling the money of his other clients.

Flo's solo career was not very successful and eventually she was broke. She had to sell her home and go on welfare. She continued to struggle with depression and drinking, and she was often in poor health. She remained in contact with Mary for many years, and in 1974 Flo even made a guest appearance with the Supremes during a concert performance.

Sadly, Florence Ballard died from a heart attack in February 1976. She was only thirty-two years old. Her funeral in Detroit was a big event, attended by Mary and Diana and many, many fans. It was a tragic end to the life of a talented woman.

A Musical Dream

In 1981, the musical *Dreamgirls* opened on Broadway. *Dreamgirls* tells the story of a singing girl group, the Dreams, who rise from humble beginnings in Chicago to become world-famous stars. At the end of the first act, one of the original Dreams, Effie, is forced out of the group because of her weight problems and conflict with the group's manager. After Effie leaves, another Dream, Deena Jones, is promoted to lead singer.

Though *Dreamgirls* was based on many different sources, it was obvious that the

Dreams were modeled after the Supremes. The musical, which was a huge hit, was directed and choreographed by Michael Bennett. Bennett had also created the musical *A Chorus Line* and was a big Supremes fan.

Diana expressed anger that the story of the Supremes had been used without her consent. Mary, however, was a big fan of the show. Like many Broadway audiences, Mary enjoyed the music, the performances, and incredible costumes. She thought it was a fair portrayal of the history of the Supremes and their relationship with Motown Records. In fact, Mary liked the show so much that she titled her first autobiography *Dreamgirl: My Life as a Supreme*. The book was published in 1986.

No Longer Friends

Though Diana Ross is the godmother of one of Mary Wilson's daughters, they have had a strained relationship for many years. As Mary once explained to CNN, "There has been a wedge in our friendship ever since [Diana] left the group." Mary, like Flo, had spent years frustrated at being forced into the background while Berry Gordy focused all his efforts on Diana's career. She remained angry with Motown Records for neglecting the Supremes after Diana left.

Mary's relationship with Motown became more troubled after she filed a lawsuit against the company in the 1970s. Motown responded by suing her in return. Eventually the lawsuits were dropped, but it created bad feelings as Mary started her solo career after the Supremes.

The publication of Mary's first autobiography created more tension with Diana. The book *Dreamgirl* was very honest and did not always paint a flattering picture of Diana. In later years, Mary was criticized for not writing about more positive aspects of her friendship with Diana. Mary responded by writing a second autobiography titled *Supreme Faith*. That book detailed her life after Diana left the Supremes. In the book, Mary tried to write fairly about her experiences, both positive and negative. Mary did describe times that Diana had supported her in the years after the Supremes, but it was clear that there was still a wide gap between the two old friends.

Diana Ross also wrote her autobiography, *Secrets of a Sparrow*, in 1993. The book did not address many details of her life as a Supreme. Instead, it presented a glimpse of Diana's journals and poetry. She focused on her dreams and wishes as an artist and a performer. She wrote a great deal about her relationships with her children.

Living Legends

The Rock and Roll Hall of Fame and Museum in Cleveland, Ohio, was founded in 1983 to honor musicians, songwriters, and performers

Fun Fact!

In 1985, Diana joined a group of the most well known musicians to record "We Are the World." The song was wildly popular and helped to raise money for starving children, specifically in Africa.

who have made influential contributions to rock and roll music. Artists become eligible for inclusion in the Hall of Fame twenty-five years after the release of their first records. Once eligible, the artists are selected by rock and roll historians and then voted on by about 1,000 other rock experts. To be included, an artist must receive at least 50 percent of the votes.

The Supremes were chosen for inclusion in the Rock and Roll Hall of Fame at the 1988 induction ceremony. Though Flo had passed away in 1976, there was great excitement that the ceremony would become a reunion of Mary Wilson and Diana Ross. That reunion didn't happen.

The ceremony occurred after the publication of Mary's first autobiography, and many people felt that Diana did not attend because her feelings were still hurt by the book. In any event, Mary Wilson was the only Supreme present that night. She gave a speech that thanked the Hall of Fame for recognizing the work of all of the Supremes. Florence Ballard's daughter, Lisa Chapman, accepted the award on behalf of her mom.

At the end of the ceremony, there was a big jam session in which many musicians played and sang together. Mary performed onstage that night with Elton John and Billy Joel. She was excited to be at the event but also sad that the original Supremes could not share the honor together.

Mary Wilson attended the Supremes' induction into the Rock and Roll Hall of Fame.

One Last Time

In 2000, Diana Ross announced that she would perform with the Supremes in the Return to Love tour, which would travel nationwide. Though she had asked Mary about performing in the tour, Mary had turned her down. Instead, Diana planned to tour with Scherrie Payne and Lynda Laurence, who had been members of the group in the '70s.

Diana Ross launched a new Supremes tour in 2000, but it was quickly canceled.

Mary later expressed anger that Diana had created the tour without asking for any input. Mary was offended that Diana did not ask her to join the tour until the last minute. She was not happy about the amount of money she was being offered to do the event. Mary did agree that Diana should make more money on the tour, since she had the most successful solo career.

Ultimately, Mary did not do the tour and it was a flop. The tour began on June 14, 2000, and was canceled a month later because of lack of ticket sales. Fans wanted to see Mary Wilson and Cindy Birdsong as the Supremes, not two singers who had never performed with Diana Ross before. Diana did not want to cancel the tour, however. She said, "I would sing the same if there were ten people in the audience or 10,000. I love the music and the fans, and I will find a way to reconnect with them as soon as possible."

The Influential Supremes

Despite the separation of the original members of the group, the Supremes remain one of the most influential forces in American music. With their unique combination of beauty, class, and great singing, the Supremes still have millions of fans around the world. People of all ages can easily remember the catchy tunes of "Where Did Our Love Go," "Baby Love," and many of the group's other hit tunes. Florence Ballard, Mary Wilson, and Diana Ross will be forever remembered as the wonderful and talented Supremes.

SELECTED DISCOGRAPHY

The Supremes

1963 *Meet the Supremes*

1965 *Where Did Our Love Go*

1965 *We Remember Sam Cooke*

1965 *More Hits by the Supremes*

1966 *I Hear a Symphony*

1966 *The Supremes A' Go-Go*

1967 *The Supremes Sing Holland-Dozier-Holland*

1967 *The Supremes Sing Rodgers & Hart*

Diana Ross and the Supremes

1968 *Love Child*

1968 *The Supremes Join the Temptations*

1969 *Let the Sunshine In*

1969 *Cream of the Crop*

1970 *Farewell*

GLOSSARY

a cappella Music with no instrumental parts.

acoustic Natural sound, with no electronic equipment enhancing it.

acquaintance Someone you don't know well.

audition A tryout; to perform in order to get a role.

autobiography The story of a person's life, written by that person.

chaperone An older person who watches out for a younger one.

charts A listing that ranks music sales, as in "number one on the charts."

cover A performance of someone else's song.

discreet Showing good judgment.

endorsement The act of giving approval to something, such as a product.

harmony Multiple vocal or instrumental parts that sound good together.

headliner A featured entertainer.

induct To admit as a member.

manager The person who helps a performer make career choices.

memoirs The story of someone's life, like an autobiography.

pop Relating to popular music, as in "pop singer."

racist Someone who dislikes or hates others based on their ethnic background.

R & B Music incorporating elements of blues and black folk music.

rehearse To practice for a performance or an event.

segregate To separate things, like white people from black people.

soul Music that originated in black American gospel singing.

standard A famous song that is commonly known.

tribute Something that honors a person or thing.

TO FIND OUT MORE

Motown Records
1755 Broadway
7th Floor
New York, NY 10019
Web site: http://www.motown.com

Rock and Roll Hall of Fame Foundation
1290 Avenue of the Americas
New York, NY 10104

Rock and Roll Hall of Fame and Museum
One Key Plaza
Cleveland, Ohio 44114
(888) 764-ROCK (7625)
Web site: http://www.rockhall.com

Web Sites

Diana Ross Fan Site
http://www.diana-web.com

Florence Ballard Fan Club
http://www.florenceballardfanclub.com

History of Rock 'n' Roll: The Supremes
http://www.history-of-rock.com/supremes.htm

Mary Wilson's Official Homepage
http://www.marywilson.com

FOR FURTHER READING

Gordy, Berry. *To Be Loved.* New York: Warner Books, 1994.

Ruuth, Marianne. *The Supremes: Triumph and Tragedy.* Los Angeles: Holloway House Publishing Company, 1995.

Waller, Don. *The Motown Story.* New York: Charles Scribner, 1985.

Wilson, Mary. *Supreme Faith: Someday We'll Be Together.* New York: HarperCollins, 1990.

Works Cited

Ross, Diana. *Secrets of a Sparrow: Memoirs.* New York: Villard Books, 1993.

Vineyard, Jennifer. "Doubt Surrounds Supremes Tour." *Rolling Stone,* July 12, 2000.

Wilson, Mary. *Dreamgirl: My Life as a Supreme.* New York: St. Martin's Press, 1986.

INDEX

CREDITS

About the Author

Ursula Rivera was born and raised in New York City. She has been writing about celebrities for several years.

Photo Credits

Cover, pp. 13, 50, 100, 101 © AP/Wide World Photos; pp. 4, 10, 14, 24, 32, 34, 36, 45, 46, 48, 56–57, 59, 62, 65, 76, 78, 85, 89, 90 © Michael Ochs Archive; pp. 5, 68 © Bettmann/Corbis; p. 7 (The Go-Go's) © Roger Ressmeyer/Corbis; p. 7 (Destiny's Child) © AFP/Corbis; p. 18 © Celebrity Archive Corp; pp. 40, 86 © Hulton-Deutsch Collection/Corbis; pp. 54, 71 © Hulton Archive by Getty Images.

Layout and Design

Thomas Forget